6/17

D0010712

Y

9

# What Goes Together?

## A BOOK ABOUT OPPOSITES

BY NICK REBMAN

Published by The Child's World®
1980 Lookout Drive • Mankato, MN 56003-1705
800-599-READ • www.childsworld.com

Acknowledgments
The Child's World®: Mary Swensen, Publishing Director
Red Line Editorial: Editorial direction and production
The Design Lab: Design

Photographs ©: Andrey Kuzmin/Shutterstock Images, cover
(top left), cover (bottom right); Shutterstock Images, cover (top
right), 5, 6 (bottom), 8 (bottom); Jeff Stein/Shutterstock Images,
cover (bottom left); Sonya Etchison/Shutterstock Images, 4 (left);
Blend Images/Shutterstock Images, 4 (right); Carlos Horta/
Shutterstock Images, 6 (top); Forster Forest/Shutterstock Images,
7; Studio 1One/Shutterstock Images, 8 (top); Dina Uretski/
Shutterstock Images, 9; iStockphoto, 10 (top); FrankyDeMeyer/
iStockphoto, 10 (bottom); wavebreakmedia/Shutterstock
Images, 11; Monkey Business Images/Shutterstock Images, 12
(top); John Steel/Shutterstock Images, 12 (bottom); MNStudio/
Shutterstock Images, 13

ISBN 9781503807648
LCCN 2015958144

Printed in the United States of America
Mankato, MN
June, 2016
PA02306

## About the Author

Nick Rebman likes to

write, draw, and travel.

He lives in Minnesota.

Some things are similar. Some things are different. Can you answer these questions about opposites?

Andrea has a big pumpkin.
Maria has a medium pumpkin.
Logan has a small pumpkin.

# What goes together as opposites?

Carlos has an empty glass. José
has a cold glass of lemonade.
Kevin has a hot cup of tea.

6

# What goes together as opposites?

Taylor has a green shirt. She is a fast runner. Jessica throws a ball. Rachel has a yellow shirt. She is a slow runner.

8

# What goes together as opposites?

Lee is holding heavy weights.
Hannah is holding a light feather.
Olivia is holding a green book.

# What goes together as opposites?

Sofia was on the team that won.
Mike was on the team that lost.
Ashley was watching the game.

# What goes together as opposites?

# ANSWER KEY

Big and small
go together as opposites.

Cold and hot go together
as opposites.

Fast and slow go together
as opposites.

Heavy and light go together
as opposites.

Won and lost go together
as opposites.

# GLOSSARY

**different** (DIFF-er-ent) Things that are different are not the same. Taylor and Rachel had shirts with different colors.

**opposites** (OP-uh-sits) Opposites are completely different from each other. An empty glass is the opposite of a full glass.

**similar** (SIM-uh-ler) Things that are similar have parts in common. The pumpkins were similar in color.

# TO LEARN MORE

## IN THE LIBRARY

Carpenter, Tad. *Opposites!* New York: Little Brown & Company, 2012.

*Opposites!* Washington, DC: National Geographic, 2012.

## ON THE WEB

Visit our Web site for links about opposites: **childsworld.com/links**

Note to Parents, Teachers, and Librarians: We routinely verify our Web links to make sure they are safe and active sites. So encourage your readers to check them out!

# INDEX